Casey and Maggie

by Howard Lee
illustrated by Lorinda Cauley

Core Decodable 75

McGraw Hill Education

Bothell, WA • Chicago, IL • Columbus, OH • New York, NY

MHEonline.com

Send all inquiries to:
McGraw-Hill Education
8787 Orion Place
Columbus, OH 43240

ISBN: 978-0-02-132507-8
MHID: 0-02-132507-3

Printed in the United States of America.

9 10 11 12 KOD 24

Casey's home was next to Maggie's.
Maggie was Casey's best buddy.

But Maggie had to go.
Her mom got a job in a big city.

There was going to be a block party for Maggie's family.

Casey was sad to see Maggie go.
She was going to miss Maggie.

Kids planned gifts for Maggie.
Some shopped for gifts.
Some made gifts.

Casey could not shop for a gift.
She had only ten pennies in her piggy bank.

What could Casey create for Maggie?
Casey had to think.
What did Maggie like?

Casey looked at Maggie.
It helped Casey think of memories.

Maggie sang on key.
Maggie danced to the beat.

Maggie liked to skate on concrete.
Maggie skated fast, even with pads.

Maggie liked to see homes go up.
She liked to see trucks on the street.

Maggie liked the circus.

Here, Maggie was smiling at the funny man.

These ideas helped Casey with her gift.
It seemed so easy.

Maggie opened a pretty box with green ribbon.
Maggie liked her gift.